VOYAGE TO THE PLANETS
AND BEYOND

3-D SPACE ADVENTURES

The story told in this book of the voyage of the *Pegasus* and its crew across our solar system isn't real—but it nearly is. Everything in it is based on real science, and most of the technology is within our grasp. It's what could happen in the future . . . and perhaps it could even happen to you.

Original story by Tim Haines and Christopher Riley
Adapted by Jenny Grinsted

BBC CHILDREN'S BOOKS/DK Publishing, Inc.
Published in the United States by
DK Publishing, Inc.
375 Hudson Street
New York, NY 10014
Text and design © 2004 BBC Children's Books/Dorling Kindersley Limited

Designed by Sandra Perry

05 06 07 08 09 10 9 8 7 6 5 4 3 2 1

A catalog record for this book is available from the Library of Congress.

An Impossible Pictures production for BBC, Discovery Channel and ProSieben
Voyage to the Planets and Beyond images © BBC/BBC Worldwide Limited, 2004
BBC and logo © and ™ BBC 1996
Voyage to the Planets and Beyond logo © 2004 Discovery Communications, Inc. Discovery Channel, logo, and Entertain Your Brain are trademarks of Discovery Communications, Inc., used under license. All rights reserved. *www.discovery.com*

0-7566-1294-2
Printed in China

Discover more at
www.dk.com

The Pegasus Mission

The spaceship *Pegasus* is powered by nuclear engines and, pulled by the Sun's gravity, it will reach a top speed of over 620,000 miles per hour. Even so, distances in space are so vast, it will take the ship 2,241 days—over six years—to visit just five of the nine planets in our solar system and return to Earth.

The two first stops on the *Pegasus* mission are Earth's two nearest neighbors: Mars and Venus.

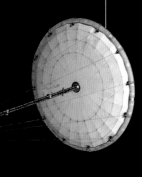

Shield protects the ship from the Sun and the planetary atmospheres it sometimes has to fly through to slow down

Pegasus is four-fifths of a mile long and weighs 440 tons.

Living areas

Power plant generating electricity for living areas

Venus

Nature: Rocky planet, second-closest planet to the Sun
Diameter: 7,520 miles
Gravity: 90% of Earth gravity
Moons: 0
Rings: 0
Mission objectives: Zoë and Yvan will land on Venus in the *Orpheus* lander craft. Zoë to remain in the lander. Yvan has one hour to collect samples, set up tests for "Venus-quakes" (like earthquakes), measure atmospheric conditions, and set up cameras.
Special dangers: Venus' surface is up to 900°F, its poisonous atmosphere is so heavy it could crush a submarine, and it has sulfuric acid clouds.

THE CREW

From left to right: Yvan Grigorev, Flight Engineer (Russian); Zoë Lessard, Mission Scientist (French Canadian); John Pearson, Flight Medic (British); Nina Sulman, Mission Scientist (British); Tom Kirby, Commander (American).

Mars

Nature: Rocky planet, fourth-closest planet to the Sun
Diameter: 4,217 miles
Gravity: 38% of Earth gravity
Moons: 2
Rings: 0
Mission objectives: Tom, Nina, and John will spend 20 days on the surface of Mars, trying to find out if there was once life there. They will test soil samples and search for liquid water beneath the ground.
Special dangers: Radiation and dust storms. Unlike Earth, Mars has no magnetic field to protect it from the invisible, deadly rays of radiation pouring from the Sun.

Days into mission: 45
Location: Venus
Briefing: Yvan steps out of the reinforced lander *Orpheus* onto the surface of Venus. The atmosphere is so thick, it is like looking through water. His suit is reinforced titanium metal with built-in air conditioning, weighing over 200 pounds.

Days into mission: 45
Location: Venus
Briefing: *Orpheus* blasts off from the surface of Venus into its sulfuric acid clouds. The porthole is made from a single diamond—the only transparent material able to withstand an attack of sulfuric acid without turning opaque.

Days into mission: 119
Location: Mars orbit
Briefing: Nina performs a spacewalk to complete *Pegasus'* rendezvous with a liquid hydrogen fuel tank. *Pegasus* cannot carry enough fuel for the whole journey, so tanks have been fired off to different locations to be picked up along the way.

Days into mission: 133
Location: Valles Marineris canyon, Mars
Briefing: Tom, Nina, and John at the 2,500-mile-long Valles Marineris canyon—so long that sometimes one end is in daylight while at the other end it is still night. The difference in temperature between the day and night parts creates strong winds and dangerous dust storms.

Sun Swing

Jupiter was currently on the opposite side of the solar system from Mars, and the quickest way for *Pegasus* to get there was actually to head back in toward the Sun, then use the star's massive gravity to catapult itself out toward Jupiter.

The journey from Mars to Jupiter took nearly nine months. Tom, Nina, Zoë, Yvan, and John spent a lot of this time maintaining and repairing *Pegasus*. Everyone also exercised for three hours a day in the parts of the ship that had half-Earth gravity, to prevent their muscles and bones from weakening. They could send emails or watch TV transmitted from Earth. Nevertheless, coping with the boredom of deep space travel was a challenge.

SUNGLASSES

The crew has to wear special glasses to protect their eyes from the Sun.

The Sun

Nature: Star—a giant ball of burning gas
Diameter: 863,706 miles
Gravity: 28 times Earth gravity
Planets: 9
Mission objectives: Fly through outer atmosphere of Sun and take samples from the star. Use Sun's gravity to accelerate ship. Activate magnetic shield to protect ship and crew from the lethal radiation.
Special dangers: Incredibly strong heat (surface temperature about 9,900°F) and light (even from Earth, the Sun can blind someone who looks at it too long). Also generates lethal radiation

AROUND AND AROUND...

Most of *Pegasus* is zero gravity, but these arms spin around the ship, creating a force equivalent to half-Earth gravity in the modules at the ends. Being weightless all the time would be bad for the crew's health.

DEAR DIARY

The crew members have private diary cameras to help them cope.

Days into mission: 198
Location: Deep space
Briefing: Zoë's sleeping area, like all the sleeping and exercise areas on *Pegasus*, is located at the end of the spinning arms, and is usually half-Earth gravity. Currently, the motor powering the arms is turned off so that maintenance can be done.

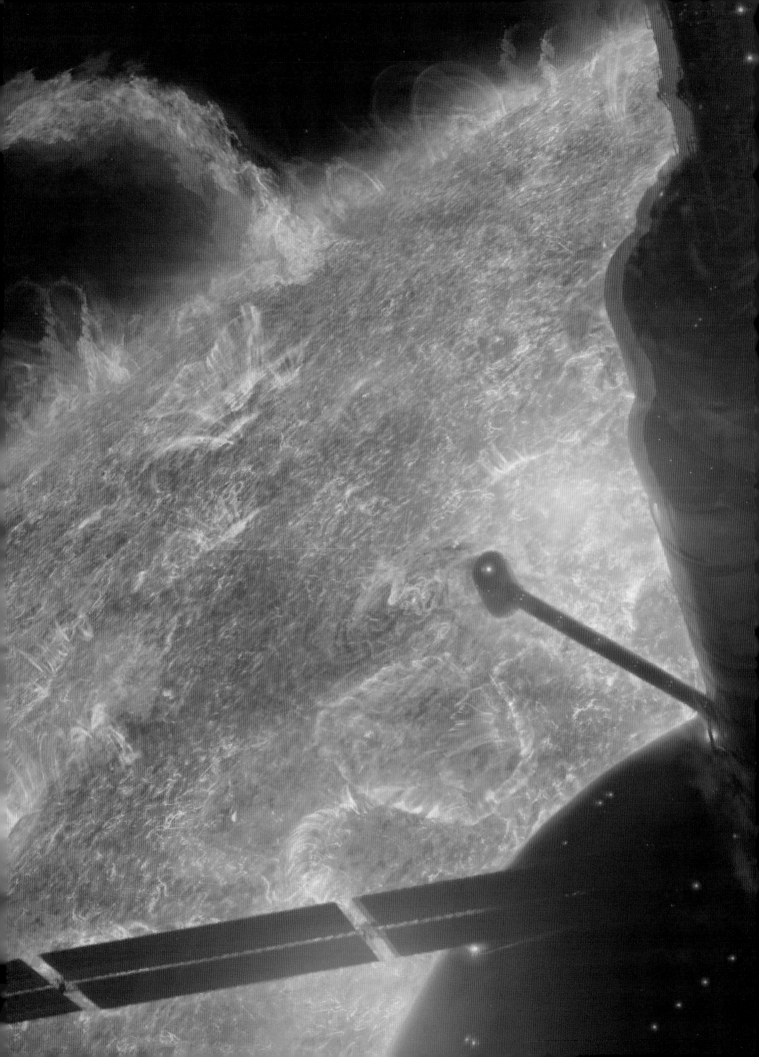

Days into mission: 203
Location: Outer atmosphere of the Sun
Briefing: *Pegasus* nears its closest approach to the Sun. A dangerous solar flare—a huge explosion of extra-hot gases from the Sun's surface—erupts to the west. If it had erupted near *Pegasus*, nothing could have saved the astronauts from certain death.

Here Be Giants

 Beyond Mars, the planets in our solar system change dramatically. The inner worlds, Mercury, Venus, Earth, and Mars, are small, rocky planets with solid surfaces. Now, though, *Pegasus* had entered the realm of the gas giants: Jupiter, Saturn, Uranus, and Neptune. These gigantic planets, thousands of times the size of the inner worlds, are huge balls of gas and liquid with only small rocky cores at their centers. They are very big—1,300 Earths would fit inside Jupiter—but also very light. Saturn would float if you could find an ocean big enough.

Saturn

Nature: Gas giant, sixth-closest planet to the Sun
Diameter: 74,900 miles
Gravity: 1.1 times Earth gravity
Moons: 30
Rings: 7 wide rings
Mission objectives: Take up position within rings of Saturn and collect samples.
Special dangers: The rings of Saturn are made from millions of fragments of ice and rock. If one of them punctures *Pegasus'* hull, the crew could be in serious danger.

Io

Nature: Rocky moon of Jupiter
Diameter: 2,264 miles
Gravity: 20% of Earth gravity
Mission objectives: Zoë will visit Io to collect samples.
Special dangers: Radiation and volcanoes. Io is bathed in Jupiter's deadly radiation belts and has more volcanoes than any other planet or moon in the solar system.

To slow down enough to fall into orbit around Jupiter, Pegasus flies shield-first into the upper atmosphere of the gas giant. The friction between the shield and Jupiter's thick atmosphere acts as a powerful brake.

Jupiter

Nature: Gas giant, fifth-closest planet to the Sun
Diameter: 88,844 miles
Gravity: 2.6 times Earth gravity
Moons: Over 60
Rings: 3 thin rings
Mission objectives: Fall into orbit around Jupiter. Release probe *Juno*.
Special dangers: Huge lightning bolts and hurricanes twice the size of Earth. Too dangerous for any human expedition to visit. Also generates radiation belts 1,000 times the lethal dose for a human.

Days into mission: 415
Location: Io
Briefing: Zoë stands next to a statue of cooled, solidified lava. In the background, Jupiter fills the sky. Her suit generates a shimmering magnetic field—as *Pegasus* did near the Sun—to protect her against radiation.

Days into mission: 412
Location: Orbit of Jupiter
Briefing: *Pegasus* releases the probe *Juno* into Jupiter's Great Red Spot—a storm twice the size of Earth. It will fly around the storm at speeds of over 6,200 miles per hour, and survive for several weeks taking samples and measurements.

Days into mission: 748
Location: Rings of Saturn
Briefing: Nina floats 70,000 miles above Saturn, taking samples from its rings. No one is sure exactly where the fragments of ice and rock came from—perhaps a shattered moon or comet.

Days into mission: *767*
Location: Orbit of Saturn
Briefing: The longer the mission goes on, the more maintenance *Pegasus* needs. Tom and Yvan are working near the main nuclear engines.

A Telescope and a Comet

The final planet for *Pegasus* to visit was far-out Pluto, the most distant planet from the Sun. It was truly a voyage into the unknown. No probe had ever visited this tiny, frozen planet, smaller than Earth's Moon. It had only ever been seen by telescope—a tiny, blurred dot.

But although Pluto was the last planet *Pegasus* visited, one final challenge remained. On the way home, *Pegasus* would rendezvous with the comet Yano-Moore—one of the most unstable worlds in the solar system.

Pluto

Nature: Mostly rock, covered with a mix of ice and frozen gases. Usually the farthest planet from the Sun.
Diameter: 1,417 miles
Gravity: 6% of Earth gravity
Moons: 1
Rings: 0
Mission objectives: Tom and Yvan to set up Michelson telescope on Pluto.
Special dangers: Pluto is the coldest surface the crew will walk on.

Yano-Moore

Nature: Comet—a lump of ice, gas and dust traveling in orbit around a star.
Gravity: Almost none
Mission objectives: Zoë and Nina to travel to the comet's surface in the lander *Messier* and collect samples.
Special dangers: Comet could break up. When a comet gets close to the Sun and heats up, the ice in it starts to melt. Gas and dust form a cloud, called the coma, around the original nucleus, and a bright tail. But the nucleus can also heat up from inside and break up without warning.

TELESCOPE

Tom and Yvan set up a telescope on Pluto that will search for heat given out by planets beyond our solar system. Pluto is the ideal location because the telescope itself must be very cold to detect these tiny heat signals.

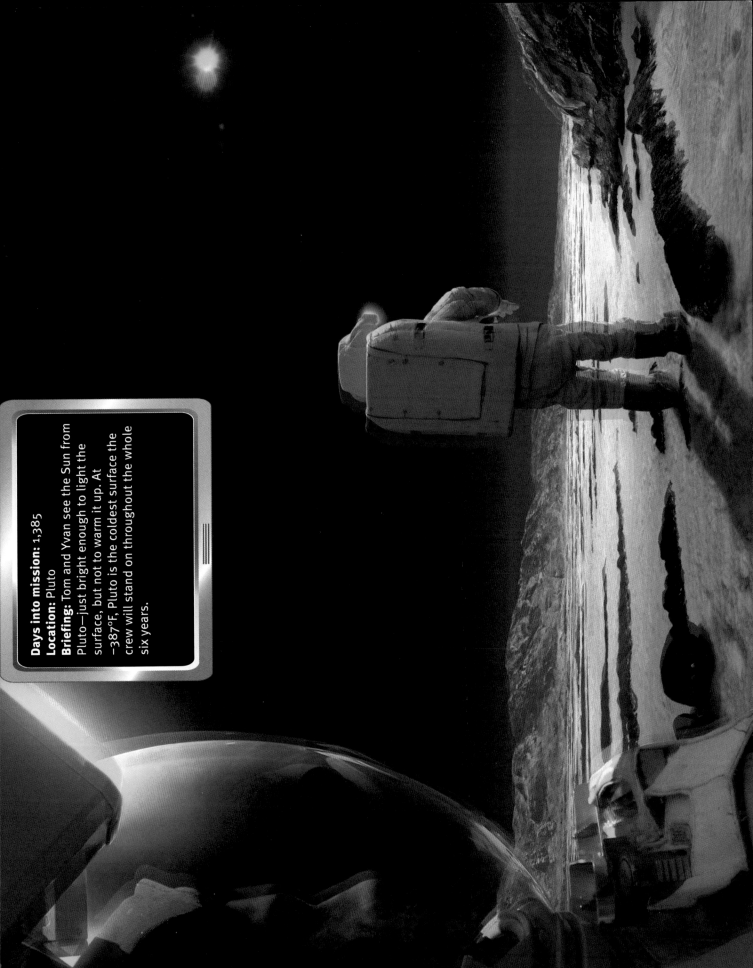

Days into mission: 1,385
Location: Pluto
Briefing: Tom and Yvan see the Sun from Pluto—just bright enough to light the surface, but not to warm it up. At −387°F, Pluto is the coldest surface the crew will stand on throughout the whole six years.

Days into mission: 1,398
Location: Pluto
Briefing: Tom lays a plaque on Pluto, the farthest point of *Pegasus'* mission. Pluto's moon Charon is in the sky—appearing eight times larger in the sky than Earth's Moon.

PEGASUS MISSION

WE COMMEND THE BRAVERY AND COMMITMENT OF ALL THOSE BRAVE SOULS WHO GAVE THEIR LIVES TO THE EXPLORATION OF SPACE

Days into mission: 2,016
Location: Comet Yano-Moore
Briefing: Zoë and Nina explore Yano-Moore's surface using jet packs while their lander *Messier* drifts above the surface. The glow is the first sign of the comet's coma.

Days into mission: 2,100
Location: Deep space
Briefing: A couple of months after *Pegasus'* encounter with Yano-Moore, the coma and bright tail of gas and dust have developed. The coma is hundreds of thousands of miles wide and the tail is millions of miles long.

Days into mission: 2,241
Location: Earth orbit
Briefing: *Pegasus* returns to Earth orbit after a incredible journey of over 8 billion miles. At first, the crew will only meet close friends and family and specially trained counselors, to help them readjust to life on Earth.